Working Out

Born in Bargoed, Rhymney Valley, David Hughes has spent most of his life living and working in the Swansea area. His poetry book *Tidy Boy* won the Harri Webb Prize in 1999. In 1992, Menna Elfyn, Nigel Jenkins and David Hughes were commissioned by Swansea Council to provide poetry to celebrate 'the spirit of place' as part of the pedestrianisation scheme for the city centre. One of the only pieces to survive the political decision to remove their work, are the words *Ambition is Critical* which are now in their third incarnation on the concourse outside High Street Station. David Hughes has been commissioned twice by Neath Port Talbot Council as part of the *Catch the Echoes* project led by Derek Cobley, to write monologues firstly to celebrate the history of Margam Park (2011), then to celebrate the bridges over the river Tawe (2013). In 2012, David Hughes collaborated with Menna Elfyn, Nigel Jenkins, and Rhys Owain Williams in a project to provide installation poetry for the new outpatients department at Morriston Hospital.

Praise for *Working Out*

'Here are poems with range and verve and vim which sometime stick close to home, in verse written in a vivid, supercharged Swonzee vernacular, or offer Republican sentiment that stays very near the knuckle. Some travel further, taking in India, West Cork or Greece or explore the poet's inner lands as he maps out an exclusion zone which denies him his own language, Welsh, or ponders what it must be like to be imprisoned at Christmas. There is experiment too, as Hughes delivers staccato burts of sloganeering, or highlights the issue of domestic violence, when the words come at you like a slap. And bird-poems too, with swifts scything through and starlings gathering in dense murmurations. But more than anything this collection, honest and true, is brightly leavened with a Hughesian humour that can both tickle the ribs or slam into the solar plexus.' **– Jon Gower**

'In this second collection from the Swonzee boy who gave the city its enduring three-word motto "ambition is critical", readers are re-introduced to a poet who takes great delight in a sharpness of phrase. The "polite rucking" at the bar during a concert's interval; the "soft applause" of a murmuration of starlings; a prison's "language of metal". Poems mined from seemingly-ordinary moments and places, with each observation elevated above the everyday by a skilful eye and sparkling wit. Elsewhere, *Working Out* is a collection of celebrations and elegies, unapologetic politics and biting satire. David Hughes is a poet of many voices, and it is a joy to see them all brought together in these pages; to hear them in these poems of Wales, the world and the points where the two meet.' **– Rhys Owain Williams**

Working Out

David Hughes

PARTHIAN

Parthian, Cardigan SA43 1ED www.parthianbooks.com
First published in 2021
© David Hughes 2021
ISBN 978-1-913640-34-7
Editor: Alan Kellerman
Cover design by Emily Courdelle
Typeset by Elaine Sharples
Printed and bound by 4edge Limited, UK
Published with the financial support of the Welsh Books Council
British Library Cataloguing in Publication Data
A cataloguing record for this book is available from the British Library.

For Ruth and Siân and in memory of Nigel Jenkins

CONTENTS

1   WORKING OUT

the train now heading east, now heading west

5   DAI THE DOG'S WELSHNESS TEST: HOW WELSH ARE YOU?
7   SHARING CULTURE
8   LIKE ROME, LIKE.
9   DANCING LESSON
10   HOW ELSE?
11   MATURE STUDENT
12   POSTCARD FROM BALTIMORE
13   CHRISTMAS RITUALS

ambition is critical

19   DAI THE DOG ON HOW TO GET A LETTER PUBLISHED IN THE *WESTERN MAIL*: A SELF HELP GUIDE
21   PROF
22   FIRST LANGUAGE
23   SLOGAN
24   GRAND SLAM
25   ON SWANSEA BEACH
26   SWONZEE IZIT?

they throw us a rope from the past

29   THE LIFE AND TIMES OF DAI THE DOG
35   *'FARRIER SIMPSON, DO YOUR DUTY'*
38   RESCUERS
40   CASUALTY OF WAR
41   MAY 3RD 1808 BY GOYA

let it run, feel the slack

45 DAI THE DOG'S GUIDE TO WELSH TOURIST ATTRACTIONS
46 STAREGAZING – ABER PROM
47 SHAME
48 DAI THE DOG – INSTALLATION ARTIST
50 SWIFTS
51 THE CATCH
52 WHAT'S IN A NAME?
53 SNAPSHOTS
55 A KESTREL
56 CARVING

this is the same man

61 DAI THE DOG'S CELEBRITY QUESTIONNAIRE
63 A MAN DANCING
64 MUMBLES SCENE – JANUARY
65 COMPATIBILITY
66 TWO PHOTOGRAPHS OF ROBERT JOHNSON
69 HANDED DOWN
70 A KIND OF HEALING
71 SESTINA FOR AIDAN
73 LIVIN
77 BIRD WATCHING
78 CULTIVATION

NOTES
ACKNOWLEDGEMENTS

WORKING OUT

A high ceiling and high windows
make him think of factories.
Banner slogans urge a greater effort
and music thumps a working beat.
Machines line the walls
with levers, belts and handles.
Screens scanned, checked, reset.

He comes each week to loosen his limbs,
lose some weight, make the heart beat stronger,
longer.

Youngsters in their tight, bright kit
flex and strut.
Tattoos tremble across tanned skin,
Lycra clings to buttock and thigh –
a pliant mould where muscles
swell and roll.
He wears flappy grey.

He rides the bike, strides the treadmill,
he hauls, heaves, sweats and grunts.
He nudges back that finishing line.

A glimpse in the mirror –
a little vanity allowed.
Not too bad he thinks, for his seventieth year.
Targets have been hit
boxes can be ticked –
he's put in a good shift.
It's time to show his card.

The one in black smiles,
consults his book,
suggests a new deadline.

the train now heading east,
now heading west

DAI THE DOG'S WELSHNESS TEST: HOW WELSH ARE YOU?

1. I am more Welsh if I:
   (a) speak Welsh
   (b) understand Welsh
   (c) have done evening classes
   (d) watch *Pobl y Cwm*

2. I am more Welsh if:
   (a) my father went down the pit at twelve
   (b) my mother went down the pit at eight
   (c) my Dadcu was born in a three-foot seam
   (d) I've heard of the miners' strike

3. I am more Welsh if:
   (a) I am the Archdruid
   (b) I always attend the National Eisteddfod
   (c) I am a member of the Gorsedd
   (d) I like dressing up in green sheets

4. I am more Welsh if I eat:
   (a) Welsh lamb
   (b) Bara Brith
   (c) cockles and laverbread (even though they make me vomit)
   (d) chicken Madras with half and half

5. I am more Welsh if I drink:
   (a) Brains SA
   (b) Double Dragon
   (c) Penderyn Whisky
   (d) until I fall down

6. I am more Welsh if I:
   (a) am the minister at Caersalem
   (b) am a deacon at Bethesda
   (c) don't go to the chapel you go to
   (d) convert disused chapels into carpet stores

7. I am more Welsh if I:
   (a) have a debenture at the Principality
   (b) know all the laws of rugby
   (c) actually play rugby
   (d) play with myself

8. I am more Welsh if I:
   (a) think Wales and England are one country
   (b) am quite tolerant of the English
   (c) maintain a frosty indifference towards them
   (d) become English so when I die there will be one fewer of the bastards

9. I am more Welsh if:
   (a) my cousin knows Richard Burton's milkman's grandson
   (b) my sister-in-law did tap dancing lessons with Catherine Zeta Jones
   (c) my brother saw Shirley Bassey in Heathrow
   (d) my father knew Lloyd George

10. I am more Welsh if I come from:
    (a) farming stock
    (b) quarrying stock
    (c) mining stock
    (d) vegetable stock
    (e) laughing stock

SHARING CULTURE

Sudhir, our guide gave each of us a cardboard box
as we boarded the Shimla train at Kalka.
Inside - a roll, a drink, fruit salad, crisps.
Safe choices for our western palates,
each bland item cased in plastic.
Cameras, bags and picnics held aloft
we shimmied past locals to seats reserved for us.

This track was laid a hundred years ago
for febrile Brits to flee the Delhi heat.
In cooler climes, the British Raj could then
rule on, without too much imperial sweat.
We settled down to snooze, to snap, to read.

Five labourers sat near the carriage door.
Their clothes dirty, their hands calloused,
they bantered like workmates anywhere.

The track gripped contours, disappeared in rock,
emerged on bridges, coiled about itself.
The train, now heading east, now west,
at a steady climb and stately pace
brought us up to clear, blue, mountain air.
One of the workmen opened a parcel wrapped in foil,
inside, a pile of chapattis,
the next brought out a can of dahl,
others had chickpeas, rice, tomatoes.
They arranged their meal on bags and laps;
they tore the bread and ate together.
As cumin and garlic wafted towards us
we opened our boxes and began a lonely struggle with plastic.

LIKE ROME, LIKE.

I yurd some clever sod sed Swonzee woz like Rome,
cozzitsbilt on sevenills.

Well I've been countinumuplike.

Firstoff airze Townill
weara wether's olwez diffrunt.
Enairze Mayill rouner side annifew carryon
ew getster Greenill;
Green cozzov awlee Irish oo cum there yurzago
(wellats wot my ole man reckns anyway).

Ravenill's onnaway t Blineymice
but I never seen no ravens up air –
few jackdaws an magpies bunno ravens.
Rose ill's up be ined Uplands
ware airza quarry up by Terrace Road.
From airsclose to Constitution ill –
now that's the sort of ill ew wooden wanter climb drunk or sober.
Annover eastside airze Kilvey ill
wot everyone goze roun wennay carn tellew somethin straight.

Ats sevenills awright,
butten airza Welsh ones
coz Bryn means ill ansoduz Pen –
Brynuvrid an Brynmill, Penviliaran Penlan.
Annen Mount Pleasant's gottoo be a ill wither name lycat.
Ass twelve ann I bet I missed some.

At feller mighterbeen good at jography
butty cooden cowin count.

DANCING LESSON

We stopped at a village taverna
beyond tourist-pretty Kavala.
Four of us on the hippy trail
with our wispy beards and smooth hands.
Locals in their working clothes stood around the bar
and stared, the way locals do.
We got our beers and sat in a corner
the way strangers do.

Someone fed the jukebox and bouzouki music filled the air.
One by one the men began to dance;
strong-armed, broad-chested, sure of themselves.
They moved sideways with a dip of the knee,
a slow, measured, crossover step.
Raised hands, snapped fingers, boots crashed down.
Arms were hooked over shoulders –
the steps quickened.

From our corner we observed and smiled
at men who danced together.
The jangle of bouzouki sizzled through the bar.

One of the dancers grabbed me, pulled me in.
The others laughed but they too had to join.
We stumbled and tripped
as our clumsy feet fumbled to a rhythm.
There was laughter as our shoulders were clasped.
We were caught up,
we were joined in.
We were dancers.

HOW ELSE?

(In memory of Nigel Jenkins)

I don't think I saw him run.

Always the careful, measured tread,
a farmer marking out his land;

and on the bike, his legs would push
that same deliberate measure.

How else to get the rhythm right?

How else to find a snowdrop
or see the clouds transforming?

MATURE STUDENT

The steady stream comes down through Uplands Square
gathering momentum from Swansea's hills.
In Gwydr Crescent, where he joins the slew
of students as they mill through terraced leats,
they become a river, young and flowing.
He is older, awkward and less sure
yet pressed to follow in the race.
Now together they pour into the park
others join from north and east,
to squeeze through gates and sweep past trees.
The river moves west, a swelling force.
He flounders, gasps, he's out of his depth;
but the youthful spate will carry him on,
it's uplifting and strong, will keep him afloat.

POSTCARD FROM BALTIMORE, WEST CORK SEPTEMBER 14TH 2001

Civilised place this
though it's had its share of pain:
raided by pirates, people taken for slaves;
when the famine came
there were too many dead to bury,
five miles away in Skibbereen.

Walked to the Beacon -
big skies, the sea blue and empty.
Watched as the sun lowered into the ocean,
and a wind rose from the west.
Stood on the cliff's edge,
looked to America.

CHRISTMAS RITUALS

Brangwyn's panels glow around us,
the imperial pageant parades across the walls.
Exotic, lush and beautifully, hopelessly out of date.
We reflect their pastel shades and perhaps,
some of their grossness.

Orchestra and choir shuffle into place
as we contort our way along the rows.
We nod
and smile
acknowledge
nods
and smiles
before we snuggle down to Handel.

The interval sees a polite rucking,
a deferential mauling at the bar.
Gins and judgements are cautiously passed;
we see and are seen.

After, the alto sings:
He was a man of sorrows and acquainted with grief.

> And we are back
> stepping through the gate
> within a gate,
> conjuror's apparatus,
> taking us into the limbo between gates
> where men in uniform stand with keys.
>
> Across the exposed yard
> into the main block
> and bright flat light.

The architecture is functional gothic.
The smell is of institution:
polish, disinfectant, stale sweat.
The sound is the language of metal:
stairs, grilles, rails, keys,
clatter, clink, jangle, clash.

The prisoners, in uniform,
hunch together.
They crouch forward to whisper,
they glance back, a grin, a challenge.
The Salvation Army band, in uniform, prepare on stage.
We are self-conscious in our civvies.

Peace on earth and mercy mild
God and sinners reconciled.
We hear of Christmas customs and,
God bless us all, listen to Dickens.

Christian children all must be
mild, obedient, good as he.

Here in this windowless gym,
in Swansea prison
the Christmas story is read.

The hopes and fears of all the years
are met in thee tonight.

The prisoners file out.
We share coffee and mince pies
with the other intruders.

14

We leave through the flattening light.
The doors and gates click and crash behind us.

We are conjured back
into the free night.

Lift up your heads o ye gates
And be ye lift up o ye doors.
The music takes us
and the silence before the last amen
hurts.

ambition is critical

DAI THE DOG ON HOW TO GET A LETTER PUBLISHED IN THE *WESTERN MAIL*: A SELF HELP GUIDE

Dear Sir,

I wish to express my concerns about/the Welsh language/wind farms/Brexit/the tidal lagoon at Swansea Bay/the Welsh Assembly/the proliferation of microbreweries.

Previous correspondents have failed to understand/the value of two languages/that everyone speaks English anyway/we are British and don't need Brussels telling us what to do/the impact on fish/the beauty of big propellers/it's just a talking shop/our non-conformist tradition/thirst.

This is/a precious gift/a chance of a lifetime/a blot on the landscape/a huge cost to the tax payer/an irrelevance/a chance to make Britain great again/a community asset.

Don't people realise it can/halve fuel bills/help the tourist industry/slice up kestrels/slice up cod/harm our children's education/show we are an island/be a link to our glorious maritime heritage/spoil the view/encourage public urination?

There is research to prove that/bank buildings make ideal pubs/it will cause deafness in sheep and depression in cows/it will spawn giant mutant crabs/it will make our children more aware of their identity/save us from global warming/it's a complete waste of money/it will harm employment opportunities/encourage lewd and lascivious behaviour.

People who support it are/watching our heritage slip away/financially involved/ecological fascists/in the pay of faceless Eurocrats/living in the past/related to members/irresponsible hedonists/fed up with lager.

Why oh why can't we/live and let live/stop this ridiculous waste of money/see the benefits it will bring/leave it alone/close it down/try it out?

Why don't/the Council/the Government/that nice prime minister/the police/face the facts/stop screwing us/increase investment/take a warning from history/ban it/get a life?

All it will do is keep the Taffia in well paid jobs/cause a lot of hot air/cause a lot of cold air/cause flooding in Mumbles/generate huge profits for overseas investors/encourage undesirable elements into our law-abiding towns.

I may not know/what Cymru means/what a wind turbine looks like/where Europe is/how fish will avoid it/how much a pint of Gower Gold is/my arse from my elbow/but I do pay taxes.

I am/bilingual/Welsh and proud of it/a citizen of the world/terrified of big propellers/keen to see it expand/drunk.

I remain/optimistic/pessimistic/British/angry/sad/European/disappointed/drunk.

Yours,

Concerned of Cardiff/Rabid of Rhos/Parched of Ponty/a true Welshman and an expert on wind.

PROF

E woz clever so Terry called im Prof.
Eed talkbout anythin overra pint.
Knew allsorts bout politics annat stuff,
spentages chopsin, splainin wotty meant.
Workimself uppywood an starter shout
butty didn mean no arm, an slongzy
kep to a cupla sherbets eed be orrite.
Butten e vanished frommer pub – from Swonzee.
Terry tole me later eed lossiz flat
cozzeed started drinkin evvy. Ad to sleep
onner beach – anninawinter, ass nogreat.
E woz drinkin at wite cider, roughen cheap.
Someone founim drownded arfra storm.

Prof woz orrite – e never meant no arm.

FIRST LANGUAGE

The damage is done but still I pine;
for me the thread was snapped,
Welsh words are and are not mine.

The decision made was thought benign:
one language would be scrapped.
The damage is done but still I pine.

My mother's tongue would not be mine,
another spring would not be tapped.
Welsh words are and are not mine.

Two tongues twisted would not align,
the future plainly mapped.
The damage was done but still I pine.

I can say *bore da,* pronounce *y waun,*
but the flow is securely capped.
Welsh words are and are not mine.

I did what I could to restore the line
but memory and tongue were trapped;
the damage was done, so still I pine.
Welsh words are and are not mine.

SLOGAN

my name is legion three is a crowd two is company one is one and all alone
a woman's work is never done man is born unto trouble is my middle name
reality is hard war is hell is other people black is beautiful west is best the east is red
ownership is nine tenths of the law property is theft history is bunk
the novel is dead the past is another country April is the cruellest month
spring is sprung summer is ycummen in
yesterday is gone the day is lost the night is young tomorrow is another day
revenge is sweet vengeance is mine sorry is the hardest word
Elvis is King Clapton is God is love is all you need
Wayne is gay Gav is lush speech is silver silence is golden
the truth is out there beauty is truth
blood is thicker than water is life is sweet
flesh is grass death is final
but

ambition is critical

GRAND SLAM

Tried to run
closed down
took a big hit.

Ruck formed
arm caught
boot goes in.

Cracked ribs
smashed nose
lot of blood.

In the wrong place
shouldn't have been in my way
shouldn't have said that.

Asking for it
wasn't she?

ON SWANSEA BEACH

Detector wielding treasure seekers,
schoolkids out with their teachers,
office lunchbreak sandwich eaters,
(for thirty minutes, treadmill cheaters);
amblers, strollers, trotters, dashers,
sidlers, stalkers, creepers, flashers,
breathless, red-faced, stumbling joggers,
breathless, red-faced, fumbling snoggers;
telescope-toting, bird-mad twitchers,
cigarette-sucking, school-hating mitchers,
fundamentalists armed with banners,
solitary horizon scanners;
arty-farty photograph takers,
happy snapping holiday makers,
castle creating engineers,
mothers harassed, babies in tears;
whizzing Frisbees, balls and bats –
slaps and tears, family spats,
the lads who laugh, the lads who fight,
dogs that bark, dogs that bite;
sunbathers coyly starting to strip,
while the brave or mad are planning a dip,
leering boys, giggling girls –
windblown skirts, windblown curls;
the isolated, distant figure,
the driftwood, shell and pebble picker,
soaring, twisting, streaming kites,
the homeless seeking a place for the night;
lovers running hand in hand,
lovers writing *LOVE* in sand.

The mums, the dads, the dogs, the lovers,
the perverts, the walkers and the runners,
the happy, the homeless, you and me –
all returning, tugged back to the sea.

SWONZEE IZIT?

There and Back
Swansea's Cape Horners fully laden
sailed through sunshine, storm and spray;
anthracite to Valparaiso –
copper ore to Fabian's Bay.

High tide rainy day riddles
Tell me this and you'll have money to spend,
where does the sea begin and the river end?
Tell me this and I'll give you gold for tin,
where does the sea end and the sky begin?

Local Weather Lore
Wenew lookser crosser water
anner Devon coassiz plain,
thenew bettew bottom dollar
ew woan av longter wafer rain.

Few look an carn see nuthin,
Never mine ow ard ew frown,
thenew better putew mac on
cozits awready pissin down.

Eyetalian Cnection
Swonzee's gotter bay like Naples,
spilt on sevenills like Rome,
buttonless they got ower rainfall
Itlee canever be like ome.

Talkin Erritidge
A: Ew know at Esseltine?
B: At Tory withy air slicked back?
A: E woz born yurrin Swonzee.
B: Funny – e doan soun liker cowin Jack.

A: But en, it woz Uplands –
B: Ats ware sex is wotter coal cumzin.

they throw us a rope from the past

THE LIFE AND TIMES OF DAI THE DOG

Dai the Dog explains his pedigree and describes
himself with characteristic modesty

My bloodline stretches over Wales,
a cocktail of *hwntws* and *gog*,
a splash from the west, a dash from Gwent -
I'm a pure bred mongrel dog.

I'm a rural urban sheepdog
with one eye the colour of milk,
the other as bright as the evening star
and my coat's as smooth as silk.

I'm quicker than a greyhound;
I've got what some call grit.
My teeth are long and sharp
and whatever I bite stays bit.

Dai the Dog's republican sentiments are expressed in terms of dislike
for some of his fellow Welsh canines.

'I've never thought much of corgis' growled Dai,
'since I saw some on a TV screen
wagging their tails at Windsor
and licking the hand of a queen.'

Dai the Dog looks at Swansea Bay and contemplates
the strangeness of humans

'What is it about humans?', mused Dai,
as he sniffed at a rotting dap,
'why will they not let me shit on the beach,
when the sea is full of their crap.'

*Dai the Dog looks wistfully across the Irish Sea
and ruminates on the quirks of geography*

Despite Ireland's pain and trouble
despite the sorrow and ills,
the sea makes a better border
than a river and some hills.

*Dai the Dog delights in republican Ireland
and the importance of colour*

'What a beautiful country!' thought Dai
'No prince, no king, no queen –
and royal insignia on the post box
painted over in a soothing green.'

Dai the Dog's best dream

In his best dream, Dai does what he likes,
he does not have to wait or beg –
he lies in front of a blazing fire
chewing Thatcher's leg.

And when he tires of this
he lets out a happy sigh,
turns around and sinks his teeth
into John Redwood's thigh.

*Dai the Dog has atavistic feelings after learning
about more despoliation in Wales*

Dai heard about opencast mining
and thought of a previous life
when his leg was held in an iron trap
and he felt the skinner's knife.

30

He saw the trader with the skinner,
he saw the carcass flayed,
he saw the pelts piled high
and he saw the gold being paid.

And Dai raised his head and howled
for his ancestors' bodies torn,
for the land being ravaged now –
and he howled for humans unborn.

Dai remarks on a surprising failure in the evolutionary process

Why hadn't the Welsh evolved
with eyes in the nape of the neck?
Dai thought that would have happened –
they're so fond of looking back.

*Dai, after much thought, is sure he has found a job for life only to have his dreams
shattered by an unfeeling civil servant*

'Now I know my calling,' said Dai,
'at last, I've made a decision –
I want to dig the holes
in the graveyard of ambition.'

The clerk, smirking, asked
'What's so special about you?
Do you think you are the only one?
Go and join the queue!'

Dai the Dog airs his knowledge of Ancient Rome
and makes what he hopes will be a salutary comparison

In the Roman Empire
the plebs, it is said,
were kept in check
with circuses and bread.

The theory's the same now
I'm sure you realise,
only today we have the House of Windsor
and a Big Mac with fries.

Dai the Dog welcomes the proposal to modernise the House of Lords and, having
made a happy but obvious discovery, wishes to celebrate the development of the
democratic process with a minimalist poem.

Ermine rhymes with vermin

On finding a copy of Tony Blair's 'Journey', Dai the Dog was intrigued to find a
reference to devolution as a 'dangerous game' and spent some time speculating on
what 'the modest one' meant by these words

Did he mean 'game' as in grouse?
(The kind toffs like to shoot)
Or was it game as in poker
or perhaps Trivial Pursuit.

Did he mean dangerous as in Abu Ghraib?
Or as in IEDs?
Was it dangerous as in liaisons
Or as in WMDs?

*Dai the Dog is deeply depressed at certain intelligence
concerning the BBC News anchor.*

Oh Huw, Huw, what have you done?
This is the news we were dreading –
a Welshman's got the gig
to commentate at a royal wedding.

Your lilting voice will celebrate
the flummery, trash and tawdry.
You could have refused, remained a man
but now you're just a corgi.

*Reflecting on the ubiquitous poster,
Dai has clear advice on how best
to 'Help the Heroes'*

Stop voting for the politicians,
who without just cause,
want us to fight
old men's illegal wars.

*Dai, who for years, had struggled with the concept of
'the trickle down effect' as applied to financial
investment in the south-east of England
and its supposed benefit to Wales,
has a eureka moment while attending
to a call of nature.*

Dai's piss trickled down the post
a trickle of golden rain,
it trickled down the gutter,
before trickling down the drain.

33

*Dai gives vent to his feelings on the badge chosen
by the Welsh Rugby Union and gives historic reasons
why it should go.*

It is time to drop the three white feathers,
they have no relevance or purpose.
Must the WRU be reminded it is the badge
of a very long line of usurpers.

'FARRIER SIMPSON, DO YOUR DUTY'

I did not see him
but the manner of that duty
is to swing the cat
twice round the head
give a stroke
draw the tails through the fingers
to rid them of skin
flesh or blood,
and then come on again.

I did not see him
but an astounding sensation
went to my toenails
went to my fingernails
stung me to the heart
a knife through my body.

ONE

It would be kind Simpson not to strike me on the same place again

TWO

Again, on the right shoulder blade

THREE

Again, on the left.

FOUR

I felt my flesh quiver in every nerve.
The time between each stroke agonising
yet the next came too soon.

  FIVE

One fortieth part.

The time between each stroke, agonising.

                                  TWENTY FIVE

The time between each stroke, agonising.

                                        FIFTY

I felt I had lived my life
in pain and torture.
Time when existence had pleasure
was a dream
long
long
gone by.

Strokes not so sharp
blows of heavy weights.
More painful.
Slower.

Quicker Simpson.
Let it be done.
You are very slow!

I felt I could yield,
beg forgiveness.
But not from them
not them.
But I prayed to God
to put it in their minds
to stop.

The time between each stroke, agonising.

ONE HUNDRED

The officer said:

Take him down, he is a young soldier.

RESCUERS

In praise of local historians
For ER, JW and RC

'The past is not a millstone but a life raft' Paul Durcan

They pester neighbours,
note their memories,
translate family ramblings;
prowl archives,
blow dust off registers,
get tangled in the internet.

They climb the branches of family trees,
root out parents,
uncover children;
haunt cemeteries,
scrape lichen, gouge out moss,
reveal *'The Beloved Wife'*.

They discover where the pilgrims walked,
where the washing was done,
and the stone quarried;
where the Welfare stood,
where the dances were held
and the bands that played.

They list the servants at Ty Mawr,
the names of those who went to war
and those who stayed.

They know where the trains ran,
and when they stopped.
They mark the last mine.

They wander purposefully,
wondering why?
Why there? Why then?

They nudge councils,
needle developers,
make planners revise plans.

They throw us a rope from the past,
reminding us who we are –
they make rafts.

CASUALTY OF WAR

in memory of Mattie Rees

In prosperous Carmarthen town
apprenticed to a milliner,
she stretched felt, stitched feathers to the crown
of hats she made for lawyers' wives,
for the daughters of farmers to flaunt
in chapel – tokens of their tidy lives.

Pretty and with no care
for the lovelorn men itching in serge
who waited and hoped in Nott Square,
as she passed on the arm of another.

Nineteen forty and redundancy;
Carmarthen ladies had to improvise,
Mattie's hats – a luxury.
So she worked in munitions, a 'canary'
making cartridge cases for 303s.
Scratched fingers, the stench of brass
and her hair bound up in a turban scarf.
An affair with the manager did not last.

The war over, her craft was outdated,
no call for milliners in austerity Wales,
and back in Nott Square no lover waited.

MAY 3ᴿᴰ 1808 BY GOYA

'O Arglwydd! Dyma gamwedd' – Dic Penderyn July 31ˢᵗ 1831

At first you might think it a blurred still from some costume drama, or
perhaps the lighting director's sketch – here the shadows, there the spotlight.
But we are witnesses to murder, a war crime, the painting of martyrdom. Not
of Stephen, accepting the stones, not of punctured Sebastian or any of that
back catalogue, haloed and meek. But we are at the killing fields.

Down right, the firing squad all bulky uniforms and weapons. Their faces we
do not see as they nuzzle into their muskets. No faces. Orders followed. Aim
taken. Duty.

Already there are bodies and blood. There is a lantern; it is when civilised
countries conduct their executions, before dawn.

To the left some people crouch amongst the dead, some kneel in the blood.
They wait for the fusillade. One man, dazed, looks up and beyond, the monk
prays or pleads, the woman clutches a bundle, a baby? A few cover their eyes.
And all the time, the central figure, the one we must look at, his shirt
impossibly white, is pinned in the lantern's beam.

Behold the man

Our man

One of us

Arms outthrust, crucified on the night.

Look at his hands, Goya insists, the stigmata. But this is no saviour, no
miracle worker. He is no hero with dashing good looks. He is one of us.
Maybe a shoemaker or haulier, perhaps a joiner, perhaps a thief.

One of us

He screams at the soldiers to look at him

To show their faces

And he screams for us, for all of us, at the guns and into the dark

I am a man

He screams

This is injustice

and the musket hammers click back.

let it run, feel the slack

DAI THE DOG'S GUIDE TO
WELSH TOURIST ATTRACTIONS

Water Sports!
Wind surfers and boats on reservoirs abound:
homes, farms and chapels beneath them lie drowned.
The Seaside!
Maritime quarters developed for yachts:
a town's identity sold off in lots.
Modern Shops!
New precincts attract big names and fat rates:
the people are moved to distant estates.
Wild Life!
Miners and quarrymen fought for their rights:
in the hills of Dyfed we saved red kites.
Conservation!
At Big Pit and Llechwedd the tourists pose:
more museums open, all the mines closed.
Nuclear Free Zone!
No nukes in Wales, proclaim it on high
while up on Epynt the screaming shells fly.
Over at Aberporth despite a few moans
The MOD is busy testing drones.
Mountain Scenery!
The rain lashed uplands are full of wild charms:
lines of pylons and subsidised wind farms.
Land of Bards!
R.S. and Dylan are ranked with the best:
Taliesin's language is laid to rest.
Cultural Heritage!
Though the heartland shrinks and the language fails
there's still rugby, some singing and BBC Wales.

STAREGAZING – ABER PROM

We come to watch this wonder
as the sun sinks into Cardigan Bay.
We come in groups and singly
hoping we are not too late.

They also come in ones and twos
until a small squadron
zooms over the pier.

From behind us, a sudden mass,
a thrilling bird cloud,
demented, elastic –
sweeps, surges and dives.

Through the old college turrets,
pink and fantastic in the setting sun,
more clouds split and stream.

Thousands of wings flap soft applause,
a chirring, whirring, susurration:
a murmuration of starlings.

The bird clouds pulse, amoebic –
now a spiral, now a helix,
at once shapely and chaotic.
They mass, seethe, swirl
in a mercurial whirlpool,
a feathered typhoon,
a squall,
a storm of starlings.

And then they drop
to roost on the pier's rusting iron.

The stage is empty.

SHAME

'a mean act'

The boy watched as his father called the horse
that grazed in the field behind their garden.
It was drawn to tongue click, soft crooning
and ragged bouquet of fresh grass.
A great head loomed, reached over the fence;
soft lips, busy as fingers, took the grass.
The boy looked up at the brown-black muzzle,
at nostrils that flexed with sudden breath;
the shocking white crescent as an eye rolled;
as muscles eased under massive shoulders,
and hooves kneaded the field's edge to mud.
The boy hid behind his father,
would not take the proffered grass
that he too, might feed the horse.

Later he went to the fence alone,
ripped some grass, clicked his tongue like his dad
and felt a thrill of power
as the horse ambled to his outstretched palm.
The huge head nodded, lowering over him
and a sudden terror clenched the boy.
He closed his fingers, stepped back
and hurled the grass at the looming head.
The horse reared and galloped away.
The thud of hooves pounded in the boy's heart
and as he ran from the fence, tears scalded his eyes.
Tears, he thought then, because he had been afraid.

When he was older he learned what they were.

DAI THE DOG, INSTALLATION ARTIST

Dai the Dog, having heard about the proposed 'Iron Ring'
sculpture at Fflint Castle, has some further suggestions for
the Welsh Government for inspired and appropriate ways to
commemorate key moments in Welsh history. Dai is rubbing his
paws in anticipation of the massive contract he will get.

Survival of the Welsh Language:

A giant Welsh Not and books painted blue –
placed in Llangennech, they might improve the view.

Rebecca:

An electrified, booby-trapped, tungsten gate
across both carriageways of the A48.

Tonypandy:

A hologram of Churchill cast into the air
above statues of truncheons surrounding the square.

Merthyr:

Twenty-four musket balls with a noose entwined
overlooking the town from Twyn y Waun.

The Penrhyn Lockouts:

The model of a silicotic lung
on the walls of Penrhyn Castle could be hung.

Llyn Celyn:

A tap with a pipe going nowhere fixed with a stake
to a raft, marked Liverpool, floating on the lake.

1984/85:

A statue of Thatcher in a golden cardy
kissing McDonald in the middle of Maerdy.

SWIFTS

Swifts
skim sweep stall swoop shoot swerve streak switch speed swipe
slip stream slipstream
spurt surge
soar

Swifts'
wings are sabres scythes scissors scimitars sickles swords
they stab snick slash
shave
slice

Swifts'
flight is steep swivel sharp switch smart swing
smooth swagger sleek spiral
sheer svelte
sudden

Swifts
are sky divers sky scrapers
shooting sable stars
are shadows

Swifts
scream screech squeal
squeeze sounds
speed
sounds

Swifts
shape skies

Swifts
are not
swallows

Swifts
make summer

THE CATCH

I did not expect to catch a fish
but took some pleasure from each whipped cast.
As the line hissed across the water
my clumsy efforts found a rhythm.
Whip.   Hiss.
Whip.   Hiss.

The line slipped through my fingers,
the sun shone and water slapped the dinghy –
until the sudden electric tug, the livewire shock
and a quicksilver streak beside the boat.

My companion told me –
let it run, feel the slack, reel in.
Run.   Slack.   Reel in.
Reel in to the arching rod.

A silveriness flittered, spattered
and convulsed in the net
until the club's despatch.
The tail strained in a last upward curl.
How quickly the silver tarnished.

WHAT'S IN A NAME?

Sgrech y coed/Jay

Yours is not the lark's ethereal call
but a rod dragged on iron rails,
a bucket scraped across a concrete floor,
the sudden rasping of a metal bar.
Woods and parkland become alloyed
with your raucous screech, *sgrech y coed*.

You're a dandy in a pink-brown suit,
on your rump, a blaze of white;
wings with badges of electric blue
and across your face moustaches flow.
Yet with these raffish looks you hide away,
you timid glamour bird, you flashy jay.

SNAPSHOTS

1953
Cwmtydu
　　We sit on the pebbles
　　looking out to sea
　　our backs to the camera,
　　maybe ten feet apart.

　　I look at this now,
　　note the gap between us,
　　know you always gave me space.

1962
Mewslade
　　That summer you really tried.
　　I was the parent, you the child.
　　I held your chin above water,
　　cheered your frantic dog paddle
　　as you pursed your lips in effort.
　　But when I let go,
　　you spluttered, sank.

　　I still do not understand how you,
　　for whom faith in God
　　was as real as breathing,
　　did not learn to swim.

1967
Pennard Cliffs
　　It must have been September
　　at Southgate,
　　the day after a storm.

　　Scrambled down towards the sea
　　taking our own paths
　　to opposite sides of an inlet.

53

Rollers funnelled into that narrowness
to detonate on rocks.
Plumes blasted into the sky
and spray glistened in every misty drop.
We watched as each wave formed.
like five-year-olds awaiting a treat.

I looked across and, like me, you were laughing,
laughing with the roaring glory of it all.

A KESTREL

quarters the southern flank of Cefn Bryn;
above the bracken he careens in languid curves,
carves arabesques.

Starlings sweep up to harry him.
In a flurry of aerobatics,
a dip and twist,
a roll on the cambered air,
he swings back to another plane.

Some small turmoil in the grass below
stalls his flight, triggers
that frantic scuffle with gravity.
Wings flail and stretch, reach out
to find the grip on air.

It holds.

The wings ease to a tremor
on the tightrope wind. For a perfect moment, he is

held

there

cruciform.

His tail
a balancing fan.

CARVING

Find the right wood –
not green that will shred
nor iron hard with age.

Look at it from all sides.
Look into the wood,
beyond the bark.

Is there something you can reach,
something to share?
Sharpen your tools.

Be bold with your blade
until, perhaps, there is something,
a shadow of what you saw.

Delve carefully now,
for deep in the wood are knots
that can twist and skew your blade.

Maybe you go against the grain,
the blade jags into flesh
and blood taints the wood.

It can happen.
Scrape it away.
No-one else need know.

That first part, the unpeeling,
sweeping slices, was grand;
you have an outline.

Now the graft with small, careful cuts,
sweat and sandpaper,
when your faults become clear.

Where you cut too deep,
where you lost shape,
you must make good with your keenest blade.

Then sand it down,
sand it for hours.
The something becomes smooth, distinct.

Perhaps it will do.

this is the same man

DAI THE DOG'S CELEBRITY QUESTIONNAIRE

The subject of this week's celebrity questionnaire is that great little country Wales:

What do you always carry with you?
History, rain, sheep and my inferiority complex.

What makes you depressed?
History, rain and sheep.

What do you most dislike about your appearance?
My weight is not well distributed. I bulge a bit around Cardiff and I need to improve my muscle tone to the west and north.

What is your greatest regret?
How long have you got?

What is the worst thing anyone has said about you?
For Wales see England.

What has been your most embarrassing moment?
1979.

How often do you have sex?
Well I was well and truly shafted in 1536 and I've been screwed several times since but none of those were consensual activities. In between times I have indulged in a fair amount of self abuse. I still have fantasies of some interesting European liaisons and more Celtic congress.

What is your favourite smell?
My neighbour's goose being cooked.

What keeps you awake at night?
Rain – and sheep – and a noisy neighbour.

61

What is your greatest extravagance?
Day dreaming about being an independent republic.

How would you like to be remembered?
As an independent republic.

Who would you invite to your ideal dinner party?
Edward I, Henry VIII, Margaret Thatcher and John Redwood.

Tell us a joke
Please see above.

A MAN DANCING

Music reached him through the booze
as he sprawled in the sun
on the steps of Castle Square.
The Latin beat embraced him
and he rose,
a man summoned by his god.

His legs moved to rhythms
languorous yet ineluctable.
With measured steps
he made slow pirouettes,
sashayed
entranced towards the band.
Arms outstretched, body swaying
he danced his graceful samba.

When the music stopped
hurt seeped across his face like a stain.
He swore, screamed,
was dragged away.
His limbs thrashed and jerked in clumsy rage
before he crumpled back onto the terrace.

But for two minutes in the sunshine
he had been David before the ark
enchanted,
alone.

MUMBLES SCENE – JANUARY

On a plastic crate
hunched forward
as if in prayer,
a supplicant of sorts,
whipped and mortified
by an east wind
slicing across the bay.

In front of him
his woollen hat,
a collection plate,
is empty.

The *Big Issue* seller
a few feet away,
maintains a polite antiphony
with the shoppers.

But the other is of a silent order,
At his side an open can
and an elegant glass goblet
from which he sips strong lager:
his chalice, his sacrament.

COMPATIBILITY

You said if you'd known I liked Johnny Cash,
you wouldn't have married me –
but you didn't
you did
and I'm glad.

TWO PHOTOGRAPHS OF ROBERT JOHNSON

(i)
Look at me
snappy hat tilted over my good eye
big smile for the women
pinstripe suit clings sweet
razor crease pants
shiny shoes.
I play even better than I look
I'm good.

I'll play at your birthday, wedding or wake
I'll play on your porch or in your backyard
in barrelhouses, bars, juke joints.
You want janglin Joplin ragtime
the preacher's gospel music
red neck cowboy songs?
You got them
You want to dance?
I'll play so you shake and shimmy all night long.
I'm good

Book me

But lock up your daughters,
your women, your wives

> *I'm a steady rollin' man*
> *I roll both day and night*

I'm the cool dude
the smooth operator

> *I am the king bee baby and you is the queen*

I'm a lady's man I'm good and I know it

> *You can squeeze my lemon*
> *you know what I'm talkin about*

Book me.

(ii)
Close up blurred mugshot
could be holding a card with name and number
doped up, hung over – someone light my smoke
my good eye's seen too much

I stood on the crossroads
bad whiskey in my belly
blues falling like hail
stared into the night
watched the last train leave

The blue light was my baby
the red light was my mind

Heard the whistle moan
heard the hellhound
felt on my neck the fire of his breath
You want blues?
I got them.

Hello Satan I believe it's time to go

Too many evil-hearted women and jealous men
too much gut-rot bathtub booze

I feel mistreated and I don't mind dyin'
It's too late to save poor Bob.

(iii)
This is the same man
the hands and fingers tell you so
his hands rare flowers, his fingers tendrils
prehensile
precise.
With those fingers he'll caress and tease you
make you think of sex and death
he'll reach inside you
grab your heart and twist.

This bluesman is shaman and lover
you listen he says
I've got things to tell you

Fix me one more drink
and hug your daddy one more time

Book me.

HANDED DOWN

My father was neat,
his frame compact,
dapper you might say.

But hands with broad palms,
fingers thick and short,
belied that neatness.

At the piano
he tutted at the limits
of their stubby reach.

But as a child
when he took my hand in his,
I knew their safe, cool, smoothness.

Long before he died
arthritis bulged at knuckle and wrist,
reshaped his hands.

Now my joints swell,
I know those shapes,
see my father's hand in mine.

A KIND OF HEALING

Blood pulsed from the wound
and the pressed bandages bloomed,
a crimson stain –
then the shock and the shocking pain.

After the blood was staunched,
the wound had to be touched
and gently touched again.
It would not be lost, that first pain.

Under the bandage, flesh binding
with sharp tugs, the wound healing.
It must not be lost that first pain,
so it had to be touched again and again.

As it shrank, the scab puckered,
its rucked edge had to be picked
so there was more blood, more pain,
and it was an open wound again.

The scab, drying out, grew darker
drying out grew harder.
Though pressed again and again,
the wound was losing its pain.

Then the scab fell away, the skin was new;
pink and just a little tender now.
Pressed and pressed again –
there was no more pain.

But the scar will remain.

SESTINA FOR AIDAN
'trailing clouds of glory'

We go to Derek and Felicity
to meet their grandson with some other friends.
The weather had been grim, but today the sun
is brightening the southward facing room.
We are a group of various ages
come to meet a special baby.

There had been a long wait for Aidan (the baby)
but his coming brought such felicity.
His parents waited, hoped for ages;
then good news to share with friends,
the ones gathered today in this room,
enjoying the glow of winter sun.

We shade our eyes from the beaming sun
to better watch the antics of the baby
in this luminous, comforting room.
Laughter, fun, so much felicity
for a long-standing group of friends –
it's true, we've known each other for ages.

We bemoan the aches of being our ages
as we let creaking limbs ease in the sun
and the sympathy of such old friends,
but our focus is on the baby
while our hosts Derek and Felicity,
bring coffee, tea and cakes into the room.

There's lively chatter in the room –
you'd think we'd not met up for ages.
Now Aidan is held up by Felicity
and beams from January sun

light up grandmother and baby.
She shows him for the pleasure of her friends.

Perhaps that's what it means to have friends,
to be able to share in a sun-filled room
the unqualified joy of a baby.
Perhaps it's been like this through the ages –
children, friendship and obliging sun,
simple unalloyed felicity.
So we hope that other friends in future ages
will meet in a room warmed by winter sun
and a glowing baby. Such felicity.

LIVIN

Ay cawlitter sail bridge
burrit look sliker knife orra feather to me.
Makes me thinker cutting through, oflyin.

Urail is smooth ancole onnew ands
an wennew clymover ew onnew own.
Vreone else goes betweener rails
annairze me ouside, goin ware I wannoo go.

I seen pitchers oviss bit ovveriver
foray putter barrage and em yots.
Innyole days, wenner tide was out
ew cd see bitsvole boats stuck inner mud
annay jess like bones pokin up.
All covered up now,
no buggerullever see um again.
Makes me feel funny
sometimes I thinkile gecaught on one vozebones
an I gescared.

I stan ryetonny edge
anner good citin feelin anner scary feelin
gess mixed up im my chest.
Annen I feel I minner bloon orrer bubble
anawl I cunyurz my art thumpin
lykit wozzan ammer.

Annen I jess step out,
Outovver bubble
an interyair.

I doan countnor nuthin
slike my body knowzitser time
an I jess step interyair.

73

Slike ew know summonle be air t catchew,
atewle be safe.

Annits slow an speeded upatter sametime.
I moutovver bubble
annoises iz rushin threwmy ed
an I sees people onny other bridge pointin –
annairze me inny air
annime fallin, annime flyin.
I'm one ovoze big gulls slidin downer sky.
I'mer divin bird.
Annen I yitter water,
oney snolike water
cozzits ard bubreaks easy.
It shakes ew bones,
slaps ew about,
stings ew skin.

I seener filmovver bullet in slow motion goin through glass,
ann I thinkimer bullet
annits me breakiner glass
annairze splosions awl roun me
like bitser glass flyin everyware.
Annen I munder.

I'm shootin down, down.
Airza rushin an roarin im my ead,
like someone turned both taps full on im myurrs,
sorl churnin an bubblin.

Anenner taps aroff.
anairze no more soun.

I nevererd quiet lykit,
slike I've landed inner boxer cotton wool.
At momen doan lars long

butiss wunnover bess bits.
No wun cn gemme yur.
I'm locked up inner water but I'm free.
No souns -
silence.
Like bein buried.
Praps its lykiss wennew dead.

Burrime nodead
Cozzime so cole my ballsisin my yurs
annis lykime inner freezer
annevry bitter me stars t go lykice.

Water's nolike water now.
Sthick, liker cotton wool is squashin
grabbin my chest
squeezin my lungs tighterntighter.

I'm nothinkin bouter cole now
coz I carn breathe annive got no breath left,
so I kick an kick.
I feel Imovin up but I carn maykit.
I'm fightin,
part of me trynter force my mouth open
anny other clampin my teethen lips tgether.
I burst outerer water liker bullet comin back
anmy lungsiz on fire
an I dunno fy should breathe innorout
annime choking n laughin at the same time.

Iffy other bitslike dyin
issiz like bein born.
Babies do come out sudden
inner squirtin wet rush.
An I feel great
lykime new annat was my first breath ever.

An I know I gottoo do it gain
Eveno evrytime I do it I'm scared shitless.

Butairze things ew knowew jess gotter do –
cozzits livin.

BIRD WATCHING

in memory of Hugh Rees DFC, FRS.

In the last few years you swore
there were no more finches;
couldn't see the stunning vermillion,
the sudden golden flashes.
I think sometimes, you didn't believe us
when we said they were about.
We could still see that brilliance
thrilling as discovery, fleeting as light.

Driving to the funeral, five goldfinches, charmed in a glittering chain
from the hedge's gloom, had me half believing in signs.

Later as we sang hymns,
a buzzard swept the valley in easy arcs.
The crows scrambled
and mounted their raucous challenge.
The buzzard, banking away,
flicked a wing for upward roll
and rose on those thermals
crows cannot feel.

CULTIVATION

'There's rosemary, that's for remembrance;'
In memory of William Treharne

After fifty years of digging coal,
you saw the garden as a seam
to tame with hard graft and rule,
where yield would match your effort.
You measured each plot to the inch,
each row a cultivated reckoning.
The soil nurtured, the crops rotated.
Sowing and planting, carefully considered
and your efforts bore fruit.

It was not just the skill,
but the hard ways too.
You crunched snails underboot,
hurled bricks at the neighbours' cats,
beat the dog with a rake.
You pegged finger and thumb
on your nose,
and snorted out
over the soil,
a swaying string of snot.
You never wore gloves when working
so your hands were bruised and cut;
you pierced a blackened thumbnail with a pin
to release the gathering blood.

The day's shift over,
blood and bruises darkened on your thin, loose skin.
Then at the garden gate,
where the rosemary bush spread,
your ritual:
a fistful of the dark green, leathery leaves

was squeezed
then, the hand, a mask over your nose.

Through the dirt, snot and blood
a whiff of incense, of oblation,
and the memory of work well done.

NOTES

Page 13 Christmas Rituals. *A concert of the Messiah at the Brangwyn Hall and a carol service at Swansea Prison attended within a few days of each other.*

Page 24 Grand Slam. *South Wales Police record significant increases in incidents of domestic abuse on the weekends of rugby internationals.*

Page 35 Farrier Simpson. *The words of this poem are taken from Alexander Somerville's autobiography. As a young soldier Somerville was stationed in Birmingham during the Reform protests in the 1830s. He wrote anonymously to a newspaper in support of the reformers. His identity was discovered and he was sentenced to 200 lashes of the 'cat'.*

Page 38 *There are many outstanding local historians. I have been lucky enough to have known these three for a long time. All have published a number of books and articles. Eiluned Rees's most recent book is 'Service & Survival' an account of the Llansteffan area in World War 1; Jen Wilson's latest book is 'Freedom Music – Wales, Emancipation and Jazz'. Rod Cooper has written extensively about Gower and his book on his home patch has the wonderful title 'A Dark and Pagan Place – a History of Penclawdd.'*

Page 41 May 3rd 1808 by Goya. *In May 1808 there was an uprising by the people of Madrid against the occupying French army. Some years later Goya painted two paintings,* **May 2nd** *showing the rising and* **May 3rd** *showing the execution of those alleged to have been involved.*

O Arglwydd! Dyma gamwedd *(O Lord! This is injustice.) these were the words spoken on the scaffold by Dic Penderyn (Richard Lewis) who was executed for the murder of a soldier during fighting in the Merthyr Rising 1831.Most historians agree that Dic was innocent.*

Page 47 'a mean act'. *These words are taken from* **Snake by DH Lawrence.**

Page 66 *There are only two, possibly three pictures of* **Robert Johnson**, *the brilliant blues singer and guitarist (May 8th 1911 – August 16th 1938). The words on the right of the page are lyrics from some of his songs.*

Page 71 'trailing clouds of glory' *These words taken from* **Ode on Intimations of Immortality by William Wordsworth.**

Page 78 'there's rosemary, that's for remembrance.' These words taken from Ophelia's speech in **Hamlet by William Shakespeare.**

ACKNOWLEDGEMENTS

Acknowledgements are due to the editors of the following:

Over Milkwood Anthology (Alun Books 2000); *Poetry Wales*; *Red Poets* and *Roundyhouse* in which some of these poems first appeared. In addition, my thanks to Jen Wilson for including *Rescuers* in the introduction to her book *Freedom Music* (University of Wales Press 2019)

Some of the short verses in *Swonzee izit?* were first seen (very briefly) as part of the pedestrianisation project in Swansea City centre in 1995. Latterly some were incorporated in the public art project at Morriston Hospital. My thanks to the curators of that project, Art in Site and Abertawe Bro Morgannwg University Health Board.

My thanks to fellow students and staff of the Creative Writing Department at Swansea University. Their knowledge and stimulation proved invaluable during and after my direct involvement with them.

I would also like to thank Jon Gower, Mike Jenkins, Phil McKenzie and Rhys Owain Williams for their support, enthusiasm and advice.

Many of us who knew the late Nigel Jenkins have reason to be immensely grateful for the encouragement, advice, time and friendship he gave. I miss him and remain in his debt.

Special thanks are due to Alan Kellermann for his astute, sensitive and imaginative editing of this collection.

Finally I would like to thank all family and friends who have encouraged me over the years particularly Gwyneth who made sure I kept my eye on the ball and my father who showed me that a passion for both sport and poetry were not incompatible.

PARTHIAN *Poetry in Translation*

Home on the Move
Two poems go on a journey
Edited by Manuela Perteghella
and Ricarda Vidal
ISBN 978-1-912681-46-4
£8.99 | Paperback
'One of the most inventive and necessary
poetry projects of recent years...'
– **Chris McCabe**

Pomegranate Garden
A selection of poems by Haydar Ergülen
Edited by Mel Kenne, Saliha Paker
and Caroline Stockford
ISBN 978-1-912681-42-6
£8.99 | Paperback
'A major poet who rises from [his] roots to touch
on what is human at its most stripped-down,
vulnerable and universal...'
– **Michel Cassir**, *L'Harmattan*

Modern Bengali Poetry
Arunava Sinha
ISBN 978-1-912681-22-8
£11.99 | Paperback
This volume celebrates over one hundred years
of poetry from the two Bengals represented
by over fifty different poets.

PARTHIAN *Poetry*

Hey Bert
Roberto Pastore
ISBN 978-1-912109-34-0
£9.00 | Paperback
'Bert's writing, quite simply, makes me happy.
Jealous but happy.'
– **Crystal Jeans**

Sliced Tongue and Pearl Cufflinks
Kittie Belltree
ISBN 978-1-912681-14-3
£9.00 | Paperback
'By turns witty and sophisticated, her writing shivers
with a suggestion of unease that is compelling.'
– **Samantha Wynne-Rhydderch**

Hymns Ancient & Modern
New & Selected Poems
J. Brookes
ISBN 978-1-912681-33-4
£9.99 | Paperback
'It's a skilful writer indeed who can combine elements both
heartbreaking and hilarious: Brookes is that writer.'
– **Robert Minhinnick**

How to Carry Fire
Christina Thatcher
ISBN 978-1-912681-48-8
£9.00 | Paperback
'A dazzling array of poems both remarkable in their ingenuity,
and raw, unforgettable honesty.'
– **Helen Calcutt**

PARTHIAN *Poetry*

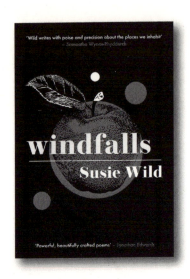

Windfalls

SUSIE WILD
ISBN 978-1-912681-75-4
£9.00 • Paperback

'Powerful, beautifully crafted poems... there's nothing like poetry to cut down the spaces between us, to leap across gaps, make a friend of a stranger.'
– **Jonathan Edwards**

Small

NATALIE ANN HOLBOROW
ISBN 978-1-912681-76-1
£9.99 • Paperback

'Shoot for the moon? Holborow has landed, roamed its face, dipped into the craters, and gathered an armful of stars while up there.'
– **Wales Arts Review**

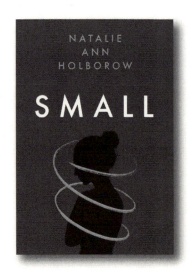